# THE GOLDEN RULE

*The Essence of Good Relationships*

DR. EMMANUEL OBI

authorHOUSE®

AuthorHouse™
1663 Liberty Drive
Bloomington, IN 47403
www.authorhouse.com
Phone: 1 (800) 839-8640

Scripture taken from The Holy Bible, King James Version. Public Domain

Published by AuthorHouse    05/29/2019

ISBN: 978-1-7283-1373-3 (sc)
ISBN: 978-1-7283-1372-6 (e)

Library of Congress Control Number: 2019906338

# *Dedication*

To my mother Dorothy N. Iwerebor, of whom it has been said oftentimes; that she walked in a shoe that most men could not even fill… She was called the powerhouse of the family, because she also took care of many members of the extended family, both near and far. May her Soul Rest in Peace.

# *Acknowledgment*

I wish to seize this opportunity to thank my wife Elizabeth, and my children Keisha Dorothy, Dexter and Tiffany, for their love and support. I also wish to thank Veronica Glen for her good faith towards me. Tawanda too. I always remember my late son Maxwell O. Obi who died in July 1998, a month before his 19th birthday. He was a Basketball and Track Star, in High School, and would have made Pro. I always asked why? but only God has the answer to man's questions, however, we thank God for the Holy Spirit who is a Comforter. May his Soul Rest in Peace.

# Introduction

The most important relationship that mankind should have in their lifetime, is a relationship with God, and by extension, with Jesus Christ and the Holy Spirit. The song *"What a Friend we have in Jesus"*, surmises the selfless relationship that Jesus has with man. The familiar scripture John 3:16 says, *"For God so loved the world, that He gave His only begotten Son, that whosoever believeth in him, should not perish, but have everlasting life" KJV.* After the fall of Adam in the Garden of Eden, judgment came upon all men to condemnation; but we thank God that Jesus left his Glory in heaven, came and sacrificed himself, to save us from eternal death, and to redeem us back to God.

*Roman 5:12, "Wherefore, as by one man sin entered into the world, and death by sin; and so death passed upon all men, for that all have sinned:"*

*Romans 12:18, "Therefore as by the offence of one, judgment came upon all men to condemnation; even so by the righteousness of one, the free gift came upon all men unto justification of life."*

*Romans 5:19, "For as by one man's disobedience many were made sinners, so by the obedience of one shall many be made righteous."*

*1Cor. 15:22, "As in Adam all die, even so in Christ shall all be made alive."*

*Song: What a Friend we have in Jesus.*

*Let us take a closer look at that old familiar, encouraging, and inspiring song.*

### What A Friend We Have in Jesus

*What a friend we have in Jesus, All our sins and grieves to bear!*
*What a privilege to carry, Everything to God in prayer!*
*Oh, what peace we often forfeit, Oh, what needless pain we bear,*
*All because we do not carry, Everything to God in prayer!*

*Have we trials and temptations? Is there trouble anywhere?*
*We should never be discouraged—Take it to the Lord in prayer.*
*Can we find a friend so faithful, Who will all our sorrows share?*
*Jesus knows our every weakness; Take it to the Lord in prayer.*

*Are we weak and heavy-laden, Cumbered with a load of care?*
*Precious Savior, still our refuge—Take it to the Lord in prayer.*
*Do thy friends despise, forsake thee? Take it to the Lord in prayer!*
*In His arms He'll take and shield thee, Thou wilt find a*
*solace there.*

We thank God; for what a friend we have in Jesus. All our sins and griefs he bore on the Cross of Calvary. *What a privilege it is to carry, Everything to God in prayer.* I remember a Radio Preacher who once said that he prays about everything, even as supposedly minor as a meeting with his students. *Oh what peace we often forfeit.* We forfeit our peace when we try to carry it on our own, by our self. *Oh what a needless pain we bear.* If we release all our problems to God, we don't have to bear the pain. *All because we do not carry, Everything to God in prayer.* Jesus, in His Sermon on the Mount, admonished the multitude in Matthew 6: 25-34,

*"Therefore I say unto you, Take no thought for your life, what ye shall eat, or what ye shall drink; nor yet for your body, what ye shall put on. Is not the life more than meat, and the body than raiment? 26 Behold the fowls of the air: for they sow not, neither do they reap, nor gather into barns; yet your heavenly Father feedeth them. Are ye not much better than they? 27 Which of you by taking thought can add one cubit unto his stature? 28 And why take ye thought for raiment? Consider the lilies of the field, how they grow; they toil not, neither do they spin: 29 And yet I say unto you, That even Solomon in all his glory was not arrayed like one of these. 30 Wherefore, if God so clothe the grass of the field,*

*which today is, and tomorrow is cast into the oven, shall he not much more clothe you, O ye of little faith? ³¹ Therefore take no thought, saying, What shall we eat? or, What shall we drink? or, Wherewithal shall we be clothed? ³² (For after all these things do the Gentiles seek:) for your heavenly Father knoweth that ye have need of all these things. ³³ But seek ye first the kingdom of God, and his righteousness; and all these things shall be added unto you. ³⁴ Take therefore no thought for the morrow: for the morrow shall take thought for the things of itself. Sufficient unto the day is the evil thereof."*

No matter how much we worry over matters arising in our lives, Jesus said "take no thought", take it to the Lord in prayer

Do we have trials and temptation? Yes, we do, every second of the day; at least just about! Is there trouble anywhere? You tell me! Sometime or the other, trouble always wants to rear its ugly head. Why? Because the enemy is always throwing his darts, looking to make trouble, looking for whom he may devour.

*1 Peter 5:8, "Be sober, be vigilant; because your adversary the devil, as a roaring lion, walketh about, seeking whom he may devour." KJV*

But the song says *we should never be discouraged*, regardless what the situation is; because we know in whom we believe, and we are persuaded that He is faithful, and able.

*2 Timothy 1:12, "For the which cause I also suffer these things: nevertheless I am not ashamed: for I know whom I have believed, and am persuaded that he is able to keep that which I have committed unto him against that day." KJV*

*Take it to the Lord in prayer. Can we find a friend so faithful?* That is the question for us as we explore our Relationships. Can we find a friend so faithful? The relationship we have with Jesus Christ is that he came to save us from sin. He came to redeem us back to God. A relationship based on love, John 3:16, *"For God so loved the world, that he gave his only begotten Son, that whosoever believeth in Him, should not perish, but have everlasting life"*. Jesus did not renege on that faithfulness, even from the time that he volunteered in the heavenly realm; when God asked "who shall go", and save the people, and he said I will go. *Who will all our sorrows share?* All our sorrows, he continues to share. We are reminded of the story of the man who was walking along the beach, in "Footprints in the Sands of Time". The man said that when the going was good, God was with him, because he saw two sets of footprints. But then, in the most difficult times of his life, when things were tough, it seemed like God forsook him, because as he looked back at the footprints in the sand, he saw only one set of footprints. But God said to him, "Son, the one set of footprints that you saw at the most difficult times of your life, were when I carried you, because you could no longer bear the situation." Not only did God share the sorrow, he bore it, at that point in time, in that man's life. *Jesus knows our every weakness.* Yes, he does. Some people are weak when it comes to lying, cheating, stealing, alcohol, surfeiting (overeating), even womanizing, or manizing! and a host of other weaknesses that beset mankind. Most of the time, it is these weaknesses that are the causes of their downfall, and destruction. *Are we weak and heavy laden, cumbered with a load of care?* This is so true of mankind, in the hustle and bustle of this life; for the poor, and even for the rich. Jesus also admonished the multitude in Matthew 11:28-30

*Matthew 11:28-30* *²⁸ Come unto me, all ye that labor and are heavy laden, and I will give you rest.*

*²⁹ Take my yoke upon you, and learn of me; for I am meek and lowly in heart: and ye shall find rest unto your souls. ³⁰ For my yoke is easy, and my burden is light. KJV*

*Precious savior still our refuge, take it to the Lord in prayer.*

Ps. 46:1 says, *"God is our refuge and strength, a very present help in trouble, therefore will we not fear" KJV*

*Do thy friend despise forsake thee?* Oh yes they do. If you're doing well, they despise you. Even if you're not doing well, they despise you still. *In His arms he'll take and shield thee, thou wilt find a solace there.* Amen. We will always find solace in the arms of God, if we take it to the Lord in prayer. Another songwriter penned the song "Safe in the arms of Jesus". To God be the Glory.

*Chapter 1*

# THE GREATEST OF
# THESE IS LOVE

1Cor 13: 1-13 admonishes us about the importance of Love in Relationships

*"Though I speak with the tongues of men and of angels, and have not charity, I am become as sounding brass, or a tinkling cymbal. [2] And though I have the gift of prophecy, and understand all mysteries, and all knowledge; and though I have all faith, so that I could remove mountains, and have not charity, I am nothing. [3] And though I bestow all my goods to feed the poor, and though I give my body to be burned, and have not charity, it profiteth me nothing. [4] Charity suffereth long, and is kind; charity envieth not; charity vaunteth not itself, is not puffed up, [5] Doth not behave itself unseemly, seeketh not her own, is not easily provoked, thinketh no evil; [6] Rejoiceth not in iniquity, but rejoiceth in the truth; [7] Beareth all things, believeth all things, hopeth all things, endureth all things. [8] Charity never faileth: but whether there be prophecies, they shall fail; whether there be tongues, they shall cease; whether there be knowledge, it shall vanish away. [9] For we know in part, and we prophesy in part. [10] But when that which is perfect is come, then that which is in part shall be done away. [11] When I was a child, I spake as a child, I understood as a child, I thought as a child: but when I became a man, I put away childish things. [12] For now we see through a glass, darkly; but then face to face: now I know in part; but then shall I know even as also I am known. [13] And now abideth faith, hope, charity, these three; but the greatest of these is charity.*

Love is the essence of every relationship. Love defines every relationship. The scripture says "*though I speak with the tongue of Angels, and I don't have charity (love), I'm just a sounding brass, or a tinkling cymbal*". We've heard the saying that "an empty barrel makes the most sound". So true! People who are empty of love, knowledge or wisdom, do most of the talking, most of the boasting, make the most sound. "*Though I have the gift of prophesy, understand all mysteries, and knowledge, and though I have faith that could move mountains, but if I have no love, I'm still nothing*". This scripture reverberates through every aspect of Relationships, especially in the Christian world. Church folks who profess Salvation; from the lowliest position, to the Pastor, Bishop, Apostle or whatever other title they carry, should naturally, have and show love to fellow Christians in particular, and fellow humans in general. This is because Salvation of the Soul readily opens the person to the indwelling Spirit of God, which is a Spirit of Love. There are many stories of non-Christians talking about a professing Christian colleague at Work, whose character and behavior is not so pleasant. The usual conclusion in such discussions is "if that's how Christians are, I don't want to be a Christian." Wow! What an irony. How about the young Christian; who after joining a Church for over a year; says that whenever he comes to church, he feels like he is in a subway car. Folks in New York may understand this better. You see, in New York, you have to look tough in the subway car, so as not to look vulnerable to other riders. Or what about the old lady who in her latter years decided to draw closer to God. So she joins a church, but after a couple of visits she stops going. What was her reason? She did not feel welcome at the church that is supposedly filled with people who profess Salvation. In Pentecostal churches, everyone is encouraged to seek their Salvation, Sanctification, and Baptism of the Holy Ghost, which is evidenced by Speaking in tongues. Most parishioners claim these three experiences, especially if they want to be active in the Church. Where is the expression of love in these instances? So again, the scripture 1Cor 13:1-13 is a great admonishment to Christians at every level or position in the church. It is said that people read Christians more than they read the Bible, so purpose to be a good ambassador for Christ, by showing love. After all, Christ loved us so; that He died for us while we were yet sinners.

*"But God commendeth his love toward us, in that, while we were yet sinners, Christ died for us." Romans 5:8 KJV*

*Charity (love) suffereth long, and is kind.* No matter the circumstance, the love is always there, constant. It's like the love that a mother has toward her child. The love of a mother far exceeds the love of a father, most of the time, anyway. That maternal instinct is a very powerful force that can transform into such physical strength; as in the case of the woman whose six year old son was pinned under a burning car, after an accident. She singlehandedly lifted the car to free her son. The pain that a woman endures during childbirth sure endears that mother to the child, and strengthens the bond and the love between mother and child. That is why the C-Section birth form is not always a good idea. The only time they should opt for that, is if normal childbirth will be dangerous for both mother and child. *Charity does not envy.* There's so much enviness amongst people, you could almost hear it. That's why there is such a phrase as "keeping up with the Joneses". People envy their neighbor's possession that they take a loan to acquire said possession, stretch themselves financially in other to keep up. *Love vaunteth not itself,* meaning, it does not boast or announce itself. It is not puffed up, does not have a chip on their shoulders. Someone who considers themself a VIP, may take a high seat at an event, and if ushered to a different seat, may take offence; then you hear stuff like "Do you know who I am"? "You better recognize"! You see these things all the time. The Word says, "...of the abundance of the heart, the mouth speaketh".

*Luke 6:45, "A good man out of the good treasure of his heart bringeth forth that which is good; and an evil man out of the evil treasure of his heart bringeth forth that which is evil: for of the abundance of the heart his mouth speaketh." KJV*

*Love rejoiceth not in iniquity, but rejoiceth in the truth.* Some people, when they hear bad news about somebody, they rejoice over that. They may not verbalize it, but they rejoice. I remember going to an Auction many years ago, and these two men were outbidding each other over an item. After driving up the price unnecessarily, one of them finally gave up the bidding, leaving the other one with a very high price tag. His comment as he walked away with a smile was "Got him good"! *Love Beareth all things, believeth all things, hopeth all things, endureth all things.* No matter how troublesome that husband is, or how troublesome that wife is, or how troublesome that child is, or how troublesome that friend is, love makes one try to bear it, and even pray for that person. Even if that person is lying through their teeth, love says to believe them, until finally you realize that you have believed a lie, all this while. Because of the love, you continue to believe anyway, you give them the benefit of doubt. Bearing it and believing, is because you are hoping for the best, hoping for the silver lining at the end of all these problems that the person has been putting you through. Because of the love you have for this person you're looking and hoping that you'll someday pass through this phase, and see that light at the end of the tunnel. It's the love, the charity; that keeps driving you. *Love endureth all things.* It's not easy to endure the pain, nor the disappointment while hoping for the best. It takes a toll on you. *Charity (love) never faileth.* It will never fail you. *But whether there be prophesy, it will fail, tongues will seize, knowledge will vanish. Now abideth faith, Hope and Charity.* It's good to have faith, *"Faith is the substance of things hoped for, the evidence of things not seen", Heb 11:1, KJV.* It is by faith that we hear the Word of God and receive it. Be it the doctrine of The Trinity; or the story of the Virgin birth of Jesus Christ; we receive it by faith. We were not there, but the Bible says it, we believe it, and that settles it. We thank God for that faith which He gave to His own Elect, and we ask that He continues to increase our faith. Hope is good. We have to keep hope alive for a better tomorrow, even for a better next minute. And then there's Charity, which is love. There are these three things, but the greatest of these is Love.

God in His Son Jesus Christ, gave us a perfect example of His love for man. It is called Agape Love, or put plainly, unconditional love; or what some have referred to as an all-consuming love. Agape love is unconditional love for oneself, and for others. It looks beyond feelings, motives, factors, or circumstances of any situation; and offers respect, understanding and compassion without hesitation, judgement or condition. It is love that is so pure, and powerful, that it makes you suffer for your loved ones. This is the love that Jesus expressed for mankind at the Passion of Christ.

*Chapter 2*

# TOXIC RELATIONSHIPS

It can be said that the degree of love, determines the level of commitment, and therefore, the nature of the relationships that we have. Also, the essence of a good relationship, is the Bible based "Golden Rule", which says to "do unto others, as you would have them do unto you".

There are many kinds of relationships, but for now, we'll look at a few...

Some relationships are **Fake**. That is they are in the relationship to see what they can get from you. Whatever they are getting, if they can't get it any more, that's it. They're gone. You are coming from a straight, clean, honest approach and mindset; you put so much into the relationship, but for them, it's what they can get. They will laugh with you, and even show up if something happens to you. The whole charade is about what they can get from you. There are many examples of that in life, with friends, and even within people's family. If they don't get something from you, next time you call them, they'll have an excuse. Some will even say "what's in it for me"? Or, as the lyric in a song said, "there's nothing going on but the rent...". Such people are calculating, in their thinking, and their motive in the relationship. Another form of Fake relationship is when both parties are putting up a front to satisfy people looking in from the outside. A perfect example is a story told by a preteen brother and sister, about the relationship between their parents. Both parents are very active in Church. Their father is an Elder, and their mother is a Deaconess. At home, the parents hardly talk to each other, except for necessary family matters. Even on the drive to church on Sundays, the one sound that interrupts the silence, is the Christian music playing on the car radio. But as soon as they get to church, Daddy is playing his Elder role, and Mummy is up and about with her Deaconess duties. They smile at each other, talk to each other, and even hold hands. Everyone in church think they are the perfect couple. Sometimes the kids wish they could be in church 24/7 just to see their parents in that mode. But the relationship is a farce, a charade. That situation definitely needs prayers and effective Christian counselling, for the parents and the children. Can you imagine growing up under those circumstances! Those parents ought to be ashamed of themselves, parading themselves as leaders in the church, and been such terrible role models to their children. Folks who do not go to church are also guilty of this travesty; especially if they are rich, influential, and highly regarded in society. They practically live separate lives, but stay together just for looks; at the expense of the normalcy of their children. How do they expect their children to have a stable family of their own, when they did not provide such an example. It is no wander that there is such dysfunction in so many families. These are examples of how the enemy tears at the fabric of society, by breaking down family relationships.

Then, there are **Fragile** relationships. It's like skating on thin ice. The result is that you will fall into freezing cold water. Fragile relationships are close to fake. In this case, it may not be for what they can get from you; but just a little offense from you, they will leave you to "fall flat on your face". There is no basis of love in a fragile relationship. Maybe they wanted something from you, that you could not provide, or they wanted you to compromise your principles to please them, and you didn't. Fragile relationships are always on the verge of breaking up; they cannot withstand any challenge, hardship, or the test of time. One of the parties may be keeping note of past offenses, thereby nurturing ill will towards the other. They are easily offended, and do not fully trust their partner. They are usually pre-occupied with what benefits they derive from the relationship, and their personal goals are more important than their partner. Generally, such people are not fully committed to the relationship, and actually do believe that they can do better, without their partner. You've heard people say "I can do better by myself", or the variation of that which says, "I can do bad all by myself". It's either because they do feel that way, or they sense it from their partner through the period of time they've been together. What a sad commentary! When there's a discussion or an argument, they stubbornly focus on their own point of views, sharply criticizing their partner, pointing finger at, passing the buck, and basically complaining about anything and everything. Even in the few moments when the partners engage in light conversation, a little jesting can set off a tirade of suspicious innuendo. Goodness gracious! Who needs this kind of relationship? Certainly no one in their right mind! Everyone deserves peace of mind. Somebody once said, "If your **mind** is at **peace**, you are happy. If your **mind** is at **peace**, but you have nothing else, you can be happy. If you have everything the world can give - pleasure, possessions, power - but lack **peace of mind**, you can never be happy". Peace of mind is priceless, so don't give up yours for anyone.

There are also **Futile** relationships in which no matter how much you try to save it, all your efforts are meaningless, futile. It's like pouring water on the back of a duck. The water just runs off. Or how about a futile relationship is like beating a dead horse. No matter how much you try, that horse will not get up and trot. Or how about a futile relationship is like trying to drive a car with no gasoline in the tank. Get the picture? Ultimately, you realize there's no point to continue with it. Meanwhile, for the one who thought they could make a change, it's been months, perhaps years of spiritual, emotional and psychological drainage, which ultimately takes a toll on the person. Leave such relationships alone. Love should never be one sided. A songwriter once made a song that said "It's so good to love somebody, and somebody loves you back". Love should be 50/50, not 80/20, 70/30 or 60/40.

Fake, Fragile and Futile relationships are in the same category. They are like a Tree with no root. All these big giant trees that we see all around, fall down when there's a storm; and when you look at the root, it's not even up to two feet. I always wandered about that. How can a thirty to forty foot tree have such short roots. One would expect that the root would grow deeper down into the ground; but because the root is relatively short, the tree cannot withstand a little storm. These kinds of relationships happen everywhere. At home, at school, at work, even in the Church. So we should make sure that we fellowship with or have a relationship that is based on mutual love. If we are in a relationship, and we notice any of these fake characteristics, we should refrain from such a relationship. If it's a marriage relationship, then the couple should definitely seek prayer, and effective Christian counselling. The fact is that people do recognize these signs in their relationships, because they can see it, they can read it. The Spirit of God in you, does give you some measure of discernment, but people tend to close their eyes to it, ignore it, or play it down. These different relationships exist in marriages, friendships, colleagues at work, business partnerships, etc. A person knows that their friend is charismatic, business savvy, and will be good for business, so they partner with the person, but only as long as the partner delivers...

These relationships are what one would call "parasitic" relationships. One of the parties is a parasite on the other, just there to suck and *milk* from the person. They are toxic, to the person. Like tapeworm or other bodily worms that are prevalent in third world countries. These worms attach their suckers to the intestine of the victim, and there, they suck all the nutrients in the food that is to be digested. These worms are inside the body of their "victim", make the stomach to be bloated, yet the person looks skinny and malnourished. They are of no use to the person; rather they suck the person dry! That is how these relationships are. The person is malnourished Spiritually, Physically, Emotionally, Mentally, etc. because they are in a relationship that is parasitic, and thereby, toxic. The person is fully affected, because deep down, they know that they are in an unhealthy relationship, but because they are so deep into it for whatever reasons, or because they do not know how to get out of it, they stay in it, until it affects them negatively in every which way. Next thing you know, they become a Fascimile of who they were created to be; a fax copy of their original self. You know what it is when you fax a document. Thanks to technology, you put an original document through a fax machine, and a copy comes forth on the other side through a phone line. But the copy is never like the original. The machine took something off of the original. That's how it is with toxic relationships. Reminds one of a song from the 70s, where a woman lamented about how she looked before she met some guy, and after going through various tumultuous experiences in that relationship, she is now a facsimile of herself that she used to know. Same could be said vice versa. Some women "put a man through a wringer", that he is domesticated and emasculated to the point that he is even not as sharp as a fax copy of himself! Lord have mercy. May God deliver us, or rather, not even let us experience these kinds of relationships, in Jesus name, Amen. At the end of the day, these experiences affect the person's sense of self', affects the person's self confidence. How can such a *one* function at work, at play, in life; with full throttle; on a daily basis. You've heard people lament about how they're half the man or woman they used to be. Why, because of toxic relationships, or in other cases, "life threw them a curve ball". Say no to toxic relationships. You don't have to tolerate anything that will diminish your value or denigrate you. If somebody is coming your way, and they are not coming right, tell them to keep it moving, and not to park it here. It is necessary to have that mind set. It's called Self preservation. Any relationship that does not confer respect and dignity on you is not worth your time and effort. Here are a few guides you may want to consider in your relationships

- How does your partner act when you're sick, or not at your best?
- Does your partner introduce you to family and friends
- What does your partner appreciate about you?
- What do they like about your character?
- Do you have friends who ask you for favors, but are reluctant to help you when you ask?
- Do your friends check in on you by their own will?
- Do you feel like you can confide in, and truly open up to, your friends and inner circle?
- Do you feel respected, trusted, and appreciated by your friends?
- If you had great news to tell someone, who comes to your mind?
- Who in your life do you respect deeply?

Relationship is one of the highest levels of love, since it is *freely selected*. As a result, you choose who you invite into your inner circle, and ensure that you are surrounded by those who love you. "You can't change the people around you, but you can *change the people you're around*."

*Chapter 3*

# FRUITFUL RELATIONSHIPS

Thankfully, there is a flip side to these Relationship realities. It is one that we should all gravitate towards. It is called Fruitful Relationships, and is the ideal relationship you want to be in. The description is self explanatory. Both parties benefit from such a relationship. It is a symbiotic, healthy, give and take relationship that is based on love and building each other up, instead of tearing each other down.

*Proverbs 27:17, "Iron sharpeneth iron; so a man sharpeneth the countenance of his friend." KJV*

*Philippians 2:3, "Let nothing be done through strife or vainglory; but in lowliness of mind let each esteem other better than themselves." KJV*

The Bible says to esteem one another. A fruitful relationship then, is the ideal and successful pattern for any and all relationships. This is what God expects from us, that everything we do or say; is to build each other up, not denigrate or disparage one another. That is what Charity is all about, an expression of the mutual love between people. Fruitful relationships have the intrinsic tendency to be durable. The members in such a relationship believe in the best for one another, and proactively cultivate and encourage one another. They do not linger on past mistakes or offenses of their partner; rather they are focused on mutually beneficial goals that elevate the team over self. As a result, they are deeply devoted to each other, are protective of each other, and have a good amount of trust, one for the other. The song "You and me against the world" is reflective of this kind of relationship. "Just the two of us, we can make it if we try" also resonates with fruitful relationships. Obviously, this deliberate decision to spur one another on, and strive for unity and cooperation, is because they recognize and appreciate how important each one is to the relationship. There will always be arguments in any relationship, otherwise the members are not being real to each other. Even in such situations, they admit their faults, apologize to each other, and even end up strengthening the bond between them. They love each other through thick and thin, and can weather any storm, challenge, or hardships of the test of time. It takes patience, selflessness, and the deliberate willingness to work together; to have this level of durability in a relationship. This might be considered "old school", but yeah, that is what has withstood the test of time. Today, the tendency is to go into a relationship with the intention of trying it out for a while, and if it does not work, oh well, let's move on to the next option. How can there be a stable Society with that mindset? But that is what we have been feeding Society, for generations after the baby boom.

James 1:8 says, *"A double minded man is unstable in all his ways."* KJV

Durability is a quality that people look for, in just about any product; so why not look for that in your relationships. Durable relationships are built on a solid foundation where the members see God as an integral part of their union, and celebrate what God is doing in and through the relationship.

## *Chapter 4*

# RELATIONSHIP WITH OUR PARENTS

What type of relationship do we have with our parents? We are admonished in the fifth commandment to

*"Honor thy Father and thy Mother: that thy days may be long upon the land which the* LORD *thy God giveth thee." Ex 20:12*

This is the first commandment with promise.

*Ephesians 6:1-4, "Children, obey your parents in the Lord: for this is right.*
*² Honor thy father and mother; which is the first commandment with promise;*
*³ That it may be well with thee, and thou mayest live long on the earth. ⁴ And,*
*ye fathers, provoke not your children to wrath: but bring them up in the*
*nurture and admonition of the Lord. KJV*

So in relationships with Parents, the Bible admonishes the children, as well as the parents. The fifth commandment is the first given relating to human relationships, and it starts with us honoring our parents. If we honor our parents, even when we ourselves are adults, God's promise is that it will be well with us, and we can enjoy a long life on earth, because if we dishonour our parents, we are really dishonouring our God. All right relationships on this earth begin with honoring our parents and having a God honoring relationship with them.

In life's experiences, there are vivid examples of how children who honoured their parents excelled in different aspects of life, whereas children who were disrespectful to their parents do not do so well. In the recent past, society can be blamed for the downward trend in Relationship with Parents. For example, television programs in the 50s, 60s and 70s honoured parents, especially Fathers. The baby-boom generation were raised in the 1950s and early 60s. Back then, most homes had two parents, and the father was the guide for the family, as well as the disciplinarian. If the father was not home, and the children were misbehaving, all that the mother needed to say, to put the children back in line, was "wait till your father gets home". TV shows like Father Knows Best, Leave It To Beaver, and Good Times (of the 70s), were reminiscent of that period. In homes where a father was not present, the mother was just as effective a guide and disciplinarian. In those good old days, the concept of right and wrong, good and evil, respect for the elders, and respect for fellow man, were taught to children from a young age. The concept of hard work, accountability and responsibility were imputed into the young minds, and it became a blueprint for their future walk in life. No wander the Bible admonishes us in

*Proverbs 22:6 to "Train up a child in the way he should go, and when he is old, he will not depart from it".KJV*

Boys were taught to be Gentlemen of character, substance and integrity, while Girls were taught to be Ladies of Virtue, and women who would help their husbands to nurture the family in the fear and admonition of the Lord.

These baby-boomers grew up during what has been refered to as the turbulent sixties. The success of the civil rights movement in the mid-sixties, though noble, worthwhile and long overdue, opened up the way for other movements; and before you knew it, everybody wanted their rights. There was the women's rights movement, gay and lesbian rights movement, uninhibited expression of sexual freedom, right to smoke marijuana; even children's rights. To make matters worse, it was during this period that prayer and Bible studies were taken out of the public school curriculum. Why? Because somebody fought for; and secured the right not to be exposed to bible teachings. As society succumbed to these rights, the fabric of the society which is woven around family, hard work and discipline, started to wear thin, and ultimately began to tear apart. By the 80s and 90s the sentiments in the music had changed, and certain TV shows and countless other commercials, ridiculed and belittled fathers and fatherhood, into oblivion. The result of the subliminal messages inherent in these programs, was that disrespect for parents, especially fathers, went to an all time high. Thank God for the many men and fathers who stayed steadfast; but many refused to stay around and tolerate the disrespect; thus and we now see the ramifications, in some children of the baby-boomers. In generation X, boys are learning to be thugs, gangsters and drug dealers, while girls are referred to as whores and bitches.

In the good old days, of the baby-boom generation, Bible was taught in schools, and its purpose impacted positively, the lives of those that had the benefit of its teachings. What is that purpose, you ask?

*2Timothy 3:16, 17 tells us that "All scripture is given by the inspiration of God, and is profitable for doctrine; for reproof, for correction, for instruction in righteousness. That the man of God may be perfect, thoroughly furnished unto all good works.", KJV*

In those good old days, the only rights that children had, were to be nurtured, housed, clothed and fed by their parents. Some underprivileged children did not even enjoy these rights, yet, as we know, history is filled with successful men and women who came from these humble backgrounds. Discipline of children by parents sometimes involved an occasional spanking, or what is sophisticatedly referred to as "applying the board of education to the seat of learning".

Did you know that the Bible endorses this kind of discipline?

*Proverbs 22:15 says that "foolishness is bound in the heart of a child, but the rod of correction shall drive it far from him", KJV.*

Granted, some parents have abused this privilege, and they rightly deserve to be punished, but we were wrong to negate this effective form of discipline.

Today, a parent stands the risk of going to jail, and a teacher stands the same risk and/or being fired, if they so much as touch an unruly student. These children know the depraved state of these so-called Child Act Laws (or whatever it's called), and they use it well. Have you ever been to any of our public High Schools recently? It's a jungle out there! How about the Middle School or even 4th & 5th grade? The gravity of disrespect and indiscipline is unbelievable. Verbal and physical violence amongst high school students is such a daily occurrence, that the government is compelled to deploy police personnel to the schools on a permanent basis. Most schools are outfitted with metal detector equipment at the main entrance, to stop and prevent the students from bringing in guns and other potentially combative metal objects. And that was long before "9/11" Now, school shootings are rampant from Primary School, through High School, to College and beyond. In essence, when society succumbed to all those rights, and took Bible study, prayer and discipline out of the school, these were replaced with disrespect, indiscipline, violence and metal detectors. What have we done to our children?

The children of generation X have been deprived of the rod of correction, which would have driven foolishness away from them. So now, we have a major population of generation X that are full of foolishness, in a lot of ways. The dictionary defines foolish as "lacking good sense or judgment". Put differently, one can say that "good sense or judgment are unknown" in a foolish person. In algebra, x always represents an unknown quantity, therefore, it is no surprise that this generation is labelled X. Some people have verbalized that the wave of tattoo-ing amongst the X generation (especially ball players, musicians, etc, who should be role models) has to be one of the most ridiculous action decisions that shows lack of good sense or judgment. There's not enough room here, to list and analyze countless other action decisions that label the generation X.

*Let us revisit those scriptures again:*

*"Honor thy Father and thy Mother: that thy days may be long upon the land which the LORD thy God giveth thee." Ex 20:12*

This is the first commandment with promise.

*Ephesians 6:1-4, "Children, obey your parents in the Lord: for this is right.
² Honor thy father and mother; which is the first commandment with promise;
³ That it may be well with thee, and thou mayest live long on the earth. ⁴ And, ye fathers, provoke not your children to wrath: but bring them up in the nurture and admonition of the Lord. KJV*

So, in the early 2000s, after about twenty or more years of ridiculing fathers, I was surprised when I saw the following two words on the side of a city bus in Brooklyn, New York – Fathers Matter – with a picture of a young man carrying his two-year old child. I couldn't believe my eyes. Since when did we now realize this fact that has been true for generations. Thank God for this step in the right direction. Relationship with God and with our parents is the foundation of a family and by extension, society at large.

# *Chapter 5*

# RELATIONSHIP WITH THE WORLD

*2Cor 6:14 "Be ye not unequally yoked together with unbelievers: for what fellowship hath righteousness with unrighteousness? and what communion hath light with darkness?" KJV*

We just talked about light and darkness, so it is when Christians have relationship with people in the world. When Paul wrote, that we are not to be joined together with unbelievers, that we are not to be yoked together with unbelievers, he was inspired by the Holy Spirit to write this for our own good. This means that our closest friend and our relationships should be with believers, and by extension, Christians are not to marry unbelievers, because one is in opposition to the other's set of beliefs. We have heard this over and over in Church; that these kinds of relationships do not work. Believers cannot yoke with unbelievers, especially in marriage. Even sometimes with believers, it doesn't work, how much more with unbelievers. For instance, if a Pentecostal who believes in Jesus Christ as the Son of God, marries a Jehovah witness who does not have such belief, there will always be problems, because that core belief is a mindset. Same situation occurs in a marriage between a Christian and a Muslim. It makes the difference between the called out one, and the not called out one; between God's own elect, and the one that is not. Without an Iota of a doubt! Somebody said it will be quarrels and arguments every day. Often, against Godly counsel, a believer will marry an unbeliever, and they bring nothing but heartache to their marriage. So, how can we fellowship with darkness, if we are in the light. The mindset makes a difference between light and darkness, and in

*Amos 3:3, it says "Can two work together, except they be agreed". KJV*

Light and darkness can never agree, believer and unbeliever can never agree, Christian and Muslim can never agree, Christian and Buddha can never agree. Thank God for the Missionaries and Evangelists who God has used to take the Gospel of Jesus Christ to the parts of the World, where practice of these other Religions have been predominant. Many have lost their lives in their quest to propagate the Gospel, but their mission has been fruitful, because many souls have been harvested for the Kingdom of Christ, although there's still a lot to be done.

Water and Oil cannot mix any more than someone who seeks the kingdom first, can be joined together with someone in the world.

*Matt 6:33, says "Seek ye first the kingdom of God and His righteousness, and all these things shall be added unto you". KJV*

Someone who does not hear the Word of God at all, is lacking in the Spirit of God and in the wisdom and the knowledge of God. The person might be a nice person, but if they are not fed with the Word, their carnal nature still rules them.

*1 Corinthians 3: 1-2, "And I, brethren, could not speak unto you as unto spiritual, but as unto carnal, even as unto babes in Christ. ² I have fed you with milk, and not with meat: for hitherto ye were not able to bear it, neither yet now are ye able. ³ For ye are yet carnal: for whereas there is among you envying, and strife, and divisions, are ye not carnal, and walk as men?" KJV*

We have to be mindful of the relationships that we form. Talking about Water and Oil not mixing, if you put water in a glass, and you pour oil on it, the oil goes to the top of the water, because the density of Oil is lower than the density of Water. Both of them are symbols of the Holy Spirit, but when you put them together, they do not mix, and when you light a match on it, the oil on top will burn, and the water that is right under it cannot quench it. When there was a vast oil spill in the ocean with the Oil Companies, the fastest way to get rid of the Oil spill was to light it up. So the oil was burning atop the water, and the ocean of water couldn't even quench it. That is amazing; really something! But if the fire is burning separately, and you pour water on it, you can quench the fire. This is a good example of why light and darkness, good and evil should not yoke. When the good is not yoked with the evil, the good can always defeat the evil, but when they are yoked together, it has no effect on the evil. The thought process is very important; it does make a very big difference in a person's life. We have to be very mindful who we relate with. We do not say that we cannot have friends who are not saved, but we must come out of the world, and not be a part of it.

*Jesus said in John 17:16, "We are in the world, but not a part of the world". KJV*

*Prov. 13:20, "He that walketh with wise men shall be wise: but a companion of fools shall be destroyed" KJV.*

That is absolutely true. The Word of God does tell us that when a person has the Spirit of God in them, even if they are of a lowly estate, God will elevate them, where they will be in the company of Princes, Kings and Queens. A perfect example in the Bible is Peter. He was uneducated, a mere fisherman, but when he was filled with the Holy Spirit, he preached on the Day of Pentecost. All the learned men, rich businessmen who came from different parts of the Diaspora, as was the tradition during festive occasions, were convicted in their mind and spirit, by the Preaching of an unlearned local and lowly fisherman. Three thousand souls were saved that day, Acts 2:41, KJV. That's what the Spirit of God does; so he who walks with the wise shall be wise. On the contrary, you've heard of educated fools, people who have Ph. Ds, and so on. Some people say B.S. is "bulls...", M. S. Is "more s...", and Ph. D, is "piling high and deep". May God have mercy on those people who say such things! Educated fools are foolish because they do not have the wisdom of God which comes from His Word.

*Dr. Emmanuel Obi*

*Ps. 14:1, "The fool hath said in his mind, "there is no God", KJV.*

So if you do not believe in God, you're a fool, no matter how educated you are. We thank God for the legacy of being raised in the knowledge and admonition of the Lord. It is a wonderful blessing. We thank God for parents who introduce their children to the Lord in their youth.

*Ecclesiastes 12:1, "Remember now thy Creator in the days of thy youth", KJV*

## Chapter 6

# SINFUL RELATIONSHIPS

*1Cor 6:18-20, "Flee fornication. Every sin that a man doeth, is without the body; but he that committeth fornication, sinneth against his own body". What? Know ye not that your body is the temple of the Holy Ghost which is in you? Which ye have of God? And you are not your own. ²⁰ For ye are bought with a price: therefore glorify God in your body, and in your spirit, which are God's" KJV.*

Once the Spirit of God is in you, you are no longer your own. Those who do not have the Spirit of God in them, or who have driven it from themselves, talk about Self-Actualization, Me, Myself and I. I am the author and finisher of my faith. But here we are been told that as a Child of God, we are not our own. *"For ye are bought with a price"*. Jesus Christ bought your Spirit, paid for your Spirit when he shed his precious blood on the cross of Calvary. God told Adam and Eve that *"on the day that thou eateth of the fruit of the tree of the knowledge of good and evil, thou shalt surely die", Gen 2:17*, so when they ate it, they died spiritually, and were due for eternal damnation; and so is everyone that has the Adamic nature. But Jesus Christ came and bought our salvation with His precious blood. For ye are bought with a price! "Therefore glorify God in your body, and in your spirit which belongs to God". We thank God for that, Halleluyah. Paul gives us good advice when it comes to sexual immorality. Run from it, he says. Get away from these kinds of relationships, as fast as your feet can carry you. All sin is evil, but sinning against your own body as a child of God, is worse because this sin is against the body, which belongs to God.

*1Cor 6:9-11, "Know ye not that the unrighteous shall not inherit the kingdom of God. Be not deceived, neither fornicators, nor idolators, nor adulterers, nor effeminate, nor abusers of themselves with mankind, nor thieves, nor covetous, nor drunkards, nor revelers, nor extortioners, shall inherit the kingdom of God. And such were some of you, but you are washed, but you are sanctified, but ye are justified in the name of the Lord Jesus Christ, and by the Spirit of God" KJV.*

Amen. See what Jesus did for mankind? Paul warns that the unrighteous will not inherit the kingdom of God, "and if we are joined with another person in sexual fornication outside of marriage, we are actually joined to a harlot's body",

*1Cor 6:16. "What, know ye not that he which is joined to a harlot is one body, for two saith He, shall be one flesh" KJV.*

Lord have mercy, things that people do out of ignorance. It is a blessing to know the Word of God.

# Chapter 7

# CHRISTIAN RELATIONSHIPS

*Ephesians 4:2-3, "With all lowliness and meekness; with longsuffering; forbearing one another in love, endeavouring to keep the unity of the Spirit in the bond of peace". KJV*

This is what we are expected to eschew in Christian relationships. We are to be lowly, no matter what position we occupy in life. Some Christians want to be haughty, they have attitude towards one another. I'm the big man around here. Who are you? You see it in the way they carry themselves. They want to sit in the front seat, and when the usher tell them to move, it's like "Who are you talking to"? You better recognize! But we're been admonished to be humble, to be of lowly character. Meekness, longsuffering, ie even when they try to knock you down, be patient, forbearing one another, ie give them a second chance, even a third chance. Now that is talking to me. I am struggling to forbear the third time. You know what they say, three strikes and you're out. One of the rap lyrics the young people listen to says "fool me one time shame on you, fool me twice, can't put the blame on you, fool me three times, forget all the peace signs, lower the chopper, let it rain on you". A third time means the person is actually trying your patience on purpose, so like they say, after the third time, it's a rap! But Jesus says to forbear. Even seventy times seven times in one day!

*Matthew 18:21-22, "Then came Peter to him, and said, Lord, how oft shall my brother sin against me, and I forgive him? till seven times? ²² Jesus saith unto him, I say not unto thee, Until seven times: but, Until seventy times seven". KJV*

That means forgiving that person approximately every 3 mins! Somebody once asked, "How about if they slap you on one cheek, do you turn the other cheek that many times"? That means the person would slap you every three mins! Who can forbear that? Lord, have mercy.

*Ephesians 4:1-4, "I therefore, the prisoner of the Lord, beseech you that ye walk worthy of the vocation wherewith ye are called, ² With all lowliness and meekness, with longsuffering, forbearing one another in love; ³ Endeavouring to keep the unity of the Spirit in the bond of peace, ⁴ There is one body, and one Spirit, even as ye are called in one hope of your calling;". KJV*

We are being admonished to endeavour to keep the unity of the Spirit in the bond of peace. So in Christian relationships, we are supposed to continue to keep peace. There is one body and one spirit, even as ye are called. We are all one spirit with the Lord, the self same Spirit of God that ministers to all of us should keep us in the bond of peace. Confusion should not be amongst the children of God. When there is confusion, you know it's the human element at play.

*Romans 8: 9, 13-14, "But ye are not in the flesh, but in the Spirit, if so be that the Spirit of God dwell in you. Now if any man have not the Spirit of Christ, he is none of his. ¹³ For if ye live after the flesh, ye shall die: but if ye through the Spirit do mortify the deeds of the body, ye shall live. ¹⁴ For as many as are led by the Spirit of God, they are the sons of God". KJV*

People are allowing their flesh to rule over them, rather than listen to the Spirit of God that is whispering to them. Christians and the Church must strive for unity and the bond of peace, and this can only be done when we remain humble, patient, and bear with one another in love. It is not so easy, but we must make every effort to keep the unity of the Spirit. Relationships takes work, and Christians have to be willing to make it work, even though people have different preferences. Therefore, we must have love, and accept one another's differences. God accepted us through Christ, when we did not even deserve it.

# *Chapter 8*

# SELFLESS RELATIONSHIPS

*John 15: 12-13, "This is my commandment, That ye love one another, as I have loved you. [13] Greater love hath no man than this, that a man lay down his life for his friends".KJV*

Greater love hath no man than this, that he laid his life for others. Jesus was selfless. He displayed the greatest love in all of human history by laying down his life for his friends. Jesus died for us, while we were still his enemies; because we were sinners when he died for us, and we were hostile to the things of God. You may not have to lay down your life in the sense of dying for others, but you lay down your life when you invest your time, talent and treasures in esteeming others better than yourself. That is selfless love. You don't lay down your life like Jesus did, but you give of your time to admonish somebody, to speak to somebody, to go and visit the sick in the hospital or nursing home, or to go and encourage somebody in distress, may be in the prison. That's laying down your life in selfless service. We want to use our talent to encourage and/or bless somebody, we want to give generously.

*Phil 2:3 "Let nothing be done through strife or vain glory, but in lowliness of mind, let each esteem others better than themselves". KJV*

Our lives consists of only a short time on this earth, so when we lay down our life in serving others, we are laying down our time for others, and we do that, not for the purpose of getting some honor or accolades for our deeds, but for God to be glorified.

*Chapter 9*

# Our Relationship with Jesus Christ

The relationships we explored so far, are what one might call worldly relationships, in the sense that these are things that happen in human relationships. Christianity first and foremost, is about our relationship with Jesus Christ. We love him, because He first loved us. So, he extended His love first. He loved us so, that He gave us His only begotten Son, and Jesus volunteered to come and redeem fallen man back to God. He knew what he bargained for; what will happen to him. He is Omniscient; knows all things, even before they happen. So He knew he will end up on the cross, and give up his life; which is why in the garden of Gethsemane, he asked if God would "remove this cup from him"

*Luke 22:42, "Saying, Father, if thou be willing, remove this cup from me: nevertheless not my will, but thine, be done.*

Even though he was reviled and hated, and many times the people wanted to kill him, he always knew; and the Bible says he would escape from there, because he knew their mind, and their intentions. He could disappear if he wanted to, but that would be the easy way out. Besides, scripture had to be fulfilled

*Matthew 26:56, "But all this was done, that the scriptures of the prophets might be fulfilled..." KJV*

The songwriter said about him on the cross, that *"he could have called ten thousand angels to destroy the world and set him free, but he died alone for you and me"*. His death was to deliver us from eternal death and damnation, and to redeem us back to God, and to eternal life. That is the love that Christ has for mankind. Christianity therefore, is about our relationship with Christ, and not so much about religion.

So, what have we done in our relationship with God? Our sins, both known and unknown, has separated us from God. Sometimes, people knowingly commit sin. They know it's wrong, they know they should not do it, but maybe the temptation is too much for them to overcome, so they go ahead and commit the sin anyway, and soon thereafter, run to God in prayer. But the sin is written all over them, and they still have the audacity to come before the Lord. God is Holy, and abhors sin so much so, that He forsook his only begotten Son on the cross, because of the sin of the world, which he took upon himself. So we run to God in prayer, "Lord please have mercy upon me"; and blame the sin on the devil. "The devil made me do it". "The spirit is willing, but the flesh is weak, have mercy Lord". But the sin is all over you. So, Isaiah says in Is. 59:2 that our iniquity has separated us from God, and our sins have driven His Spirit from us. May that not be our lot in Jesus name, Amen.

*Isaiah 59:1-2, "Behold, the LORD's hand is not shortened, that it cannot save; neither his ear heavy, that it cannot hear: ² But your iniquities have separated between you and your God, and your sins have hid his face from you, that he will not hear." KJV*

If we are engaged in sin, God will hide his face from us. So our desire should be to live Holy, so that when we go to him in prayer, He will look on us and accept our prayers and supplications.

*Ps. 145:8, "The LORD is gracious, and full of compassion; slow to anger, and of great mercy" KJV.*

God is so gracious, especially when we come to him, through the grace of his Son and our Lord Jesus Christ. Christianity is not about religion or rituals, but about having a right relationship with God. Sin has separated us from God. When Jesus took our sins upon himself, even he, had to be temporarily separated from God. GRACE is truly God's Redemption At Christ's Expense. Oh what a marvellous grace.

The Messianic Psalm 22:1, *"My God, my God, why has thou forsaken me, why art thou so far from me, and from the roars of my worrying"* KJV

This is what sin does. If you want to know how God feels about sin, look at what Christ had to suffer at Calvary. God wants to save those who repent and trust in him. He is quick to forgive us of our sins and cleanse us from all unrighteousness, and make us have the same righteousness as Christ. Well, maybe not quite the same.

*1John 1:9, "If we confess our sins, he is faithful and just to forgive us all our sins, and to cleanse us from all unrighteousness"* KJV.

*Heb 8:12, "For I will be merciful to their unrighteousness, and their sins and their iniquities will I remember no more"* KJV.

*Micah 7:19, "He will turn again, he will have compassion upon us; he will subdue our iniquities; and thou wilt cast all their sins into the depths of the sea"* KJV.

If we confess our sin and repent, God will cast it into the sea of forgetfulness. Sin is what separates man from God. God is not like man, but wants us to be like him. Some people say that you should forgive and forget. But others say even if we forgive, we can't forget. The reason they say, is that if they forget, they may be taken advantage of, again. Some would say, if I forget everything that happened to me, how would I write my autobiography? I'd have a blank page! So, I can forgive, but I can't forget. We thank God who will cast our sin and iniquities into the depth of the sea, and will remember them no more.

*Dr. Emmanuel Obi*

*1 John 1:1-10 (KJV)*

*That which was from the beginning, which we have heard, which we have seen with our eyes, which we have looked upon, and our hands have handled, of the Word of life;*

*² (For the life was manifested, and we have seen it, and bear witness, and shew unto you that eternal life, which was with the Father, and was manifested unto us;)*

*³ That which we have seen and heard declare we unto you, that ye also may have fellowship with us: and truly our fellowship is with the Father, and with his Son Jesus Christ.*

*⁴ And these things write we unto you, that your joy may be full.*

*⁵ This then is the message which we have heard of him, and declare unto you, that God is light, and in him is no darkness at all.*

*⁶ If we say that we have fellowship with him, and walk in darkness, we lie, and do not the truth:*

*⁷ But if we walk in the light, as he is in the light, we have fellowship one with another, and the blood of Jesus Christ his Son cleanseth us from all sin.*

*⁸ If we say that we have no sin, we deceive ourselves, and the truth is not in us.*

*⁹ If we confess our sins, he is faithful and just to forgive us our sins, and to cleanse us from all unrighteousness.*

*¹⁰ If we say that we have not sinned, we make him a liar, and his word is not in us.*

John is talking about Jesus Christ, whom he called the Word of light.

*John 1:1 says, "In the beginning was the Word, and the Word was with God, and the Word was God. The same was in the beginning..." KJV*

This is how John introduces/describes Jesus, both in the Gospels, and now in the Epistles. The light was manifested, and we have seen it, and bear witness, and show unto you that eternal light which was with the Father, and was manifested unto us through his Son. Everything we learnt from Jesus Christ, after being with him every day for three and half years.

John was one Jesus' favorites. He was part of Jesus inner circle of Peter, James and John. John was always around him, he is the one who laid his head on Jesus bosom. Peter was the oldest, John was the youngest. When Mary Magdalene brought word to the disciples that Jesus had resurrected, Peter was excited, and started running to the place where Jesus was buried; but John ran past him, and got there ahead of Peter.

*1John 1:3, "That which we have seen and heard declare we unto you, that ye may have fellowship with us, and truly our relationship is with the Father, and with his Son, Jesus Christ" KJV.*

John is admonishing us here, that we should have a relationship with them, who have had a relationship with Jesus, but really, we should have a direct relationship with Christ. Truly our fellowship is with the Father, and with His Son, Jesus Christ. The key idea here; is that Jesus Christ is the Son of God. In the notes given in the Hebrew Greek Study Bible, it says that man is the creation of God, and must acknowledge His superiority over him, however, man was created in God's image. In order to restore mankind to fellowship with God, He sent His Son Jesus Christ who is also in God's image, though he was not created.

In the early Church, around the 4th Century A.D there was a debate about the nature and divinity of Jesus Christ.

The Greek word Homoiousian held that Jesus was created by God, is essentially like the Father, but does not have the divine qualities of God, and therefore is not of the same essence or substance with God.

The Greek word Homoousian on the other hand, held that Jesus Christ is of one substance with God. This is in line with the biblical teaching that there is only one true God and who exists in three persons: God the Father, God the Son, and God the Holy Spirit. It is the same God, the same being, who manifested Himself as three persons. This is the doctrine of the Trinity.

Arius of Alexander refused the doctrine of the Trinity, refused to believe that Jesus Christ is the Son of God, but rather believed that Jesus Christ was created, and is not of the same essence with God. How can Jesus be equal to God, he questioned. And because of that unbelief, he and his followers in the Arian Movement, lost their way on the road to Salvation.

The difference between the Greek words homoiousian and homoousian is the letter "i", (or iota in Greek), which is very significant to *One's* Salvation. The saying "without an iota of a doubt" derives from that...so the letter "i" is what makes the difference between salvation and condemnation, between eternal life, and eternal death. So you have to believe without an iota of a doubt, that Jesus is the Son of God, and not a created being.

*"And these things write we unto you, that your Joy may be full",* when you have a direct relationship with God. *"This then is the message we have heard of him, and declared unto you, that God is light, and in Him is no darkness at all".*

The scripture says "if we are in the light, we cannot have darkness, how can you say you're in the light, if you have darkness. If we say we have fellowship with him, and walk in darkness, then we're liars, and the truth is not in us, and we deceive ourselves.

So how can we be in the light, and we go and seek help from native doctors, or obia-man, or palm readers, or tarot card readers, or soothsayers? How can we be in light, and be involved with diabolic activities, occultism, witchcraft, etc. That cannot be. We're deceiving ourselves. There are people in Church who do that. It is alleged that there are many Pastors who; because they want to build their church and congregation, get themselves involved in darkness. How can that be? What kind of a church can that be? Whatever events that take place in that church are powered by darkness. May God have mercy upon us. That will never be our lot, in

Jesus name, Amen. Churches that involve in these things of darkness are an abomination. They have no relationship with God at all.

*(vs. 7) "But if we walk in the light as he is in the light, we have fellowship one with another, and the blood of Jesus Christ cleanses us from all sins".*

This is why we must have a good relationship with Jesus, because he's in the light, we're in the light. So, if we have a relationship with him, his blood which has power, will cleanse us from all sins. The songwriter said *"There is a fountain filled with blood, drawn from Immanuel's vein"*. God is wonderful, the Spirit of God is truly all knowing, he leads and guides his people. Praise God. We have to stay attached to Jesus. Another songwriter said, *"Nothing between my soul and my savior"*. That is a direct relationship with our Lord.

*(vs. 8) "If we say we have no sin, we deceive ourselves, and the truth is not in us".*

A popular Pentecostal preacher and televangelist told his audience that when you become saved, your spirit man becomes saved, so the rest of you is your soul and your flesh. So, even if you sin in the flesh, you're not a sinner, because your spirit man does not sin anymore. Is that true? That is a fancy way to tell people if they sin as a Christian, it's not their fault, because it's the flesh that sinned, and not the spirit. He continued further, that "where the scripture says that after you receive Jesus Christ, you're a new creature, it is only the spirit that is renewed. The spirit does not sin any longer, it is the flesh that sins, and so you're absolved from that sin". Such teaching is meant to appease the people, but most importantly, is leading the people astray. This is watered down Christian gospel and discipline. These preachers teach this false doctrine in a 30min message, make audios and videos which they sell for $20 to $25. So basically, they profit from teaching a false doctrine. A Bishop has been quoted to say it's ok to love gospel and worldly music, ie it's ok to live both lives, ie you can serve both masters, which goes against the teaching of Jesus Christ who said "you cannot serve God and marmon".

*Matt 6:24, "No man can serve two masters: for either he will hate the one, and love the other; or else he will hold to the one, and despise the other. Ye cannot serve God and mammon".*

Another prominent Christian leader now preaches that you can love gospel music and other songs that use curse and offensive words. He is quoted as saying that "I love Jesus and Trap music, I quote Cardy B (a singer who is notorious for vulgar lyrics) and I also quote Corinthians, my heart mind and soul belong to God, but I do curse a little, I'm somewhere between Proverbs 31, and Boozie (a Rapper who makes songs that induce young ladies to twerk). It's okay, you can be both, God didn't make us perfect, He made us human".

Music is being used to propagate this false and deceptive teaching, because that is an easy avenue for the enemy to get into the soul of the youth. It's not ok to "live on both sides of the fence". You cannot serve two masters, you have to choose one, either love one and despise the other. That is false teaching that will lead people straight to hell, because the one that has that lukewarm faith cannot survive. You cannot have eternal life on lukewarm faith, or lukewarm actions. Gospel music is now said to have boastful and prideful words, and this is what is capturing the hearts of the listeners, and influencing their actions and behaviour.

*Rev 3:15-16, "I know thy works, that thou art neither cold nor hot: I would thou wert cold or hot".* *¹⁶ So then because thou art lukewarm, and neither cold nor hot, I will spue thee out of my mouth.*

The Bible admonishes us that if we say we have no sin, we deceive ourselves, and the truth is not in us, because sometimes we sin unwittingly. The sin nature is there even though we're sanctified, and people still sin somehow. If you tell a little lie, it is sin, if an ungodly thought crosses your mind. It is sin, but we thank God that he is faithful to forgive us our sins, and cleanse us from all unrighteousness.

*Vs. 10, "If we say we have not sinned, we make him a liar, and His Word is not in us".*

We are exhorted to have a right relationship with God.

# Chapter 10

# OUR RELATIONSHIP WITH GOD

*Rom 12: 1- 2, "I beseech you therefore, brethren, by the mercies of God, that ye present your bodies a living sacrifice, holy, acceptable unto God, which is your reasonable service. ² And be not conformed to this world: but be ye transformed by the renewing of your mind, that ye may prove what is that good, and acceptable, and perfect, will of God". KJV*

This is another beautiful scripture which reminds us that we are the temple of God. This means that we should not be involved with anything that is not of God. Our reasonable service, is to make our body a living sacrifice, a spiritual sacrifice without blemish. And be not conformed to this world, but be ye transformed by the renewing of your mind. When Saul had the Damascus road experience, his mind and Spirit was renewed. When we become saved, our mind and spirit is renewed, we become a new creature, we are born again. Jesus Christ told Nicodemus in John 3:3, ye must be born again in the Spirit, and that is by the renewing of your mind, to prove that good and acceptable, and perfect will of God. You have to prove that God has perfected his will in your life. The most important relationship of all; is our relationship with God. When Paul wrote "not to be conformed to this world", he was saying not to conform our mind and character to the world. Jesus's prayer in John 17:14-16 said:

*¹⁴ I have given them thy word; and the world hath hated them, because they are not of the world, even as I am not of the world. ¹⁵ I pray not that thou shouldest take them out of the world, but that thou shouldest keep them from the evil. ¹⁶ They are not of the world, even as I am not of the world", KJV.*

God created man to have a good relationship with Him, but when Adam and Eve sinned, they destroyed that relationship. God is Omniscient, and knew that this will happen; so He had a plan B, which involved sending his only begotten Son to die for us, so that we might be restored to a right relationship with Him. God had always intended that his people should live in a right relationship with him. This relationship is described in terms of a *covenant*. He gave them the commandments to guide them into a right relationship with God and to one another. The purpose of these laws was to convert the sinful soul. Again and again we read in the Old Testament how they did not obey these laws. Disaster came as a result. Occasionally there seemed to be hope, when they recommitted themselves to the covenant relationship with God, but soon, they fell back to their sinful ways.

Human beings are created with a hunger to live in a right relationship with God. Until we experience this relationship there is always a spiritual hunger that is unsatisfied. When we come into a right relationship with God we find the purpose and meaning of our lives.

The good news (gospel) is that God has enabled us to live in this right relationship with him. This righteousness comes from God. It is his gift to us. We cannot earn it. We receive it 'by faith'. We no longer live under guilt and condemnation, and nothing can separate us from the love of God (Romans 8:1–39).

Righteousness means a right relationship with God, which leads to right relationships with others, and this is made possible through the life, death and resurrection of Jesus.

Lord, we thank you that through the life, death and resurrection of Jesus Christ, you make it possible for us to have a right relationship with you and, through that, also to have right relationships with others. Thank you that we cannot earn it, but receive it as a gift by faith. Help us today to walk in that relationship with you. Help us also to do all in our power to pass on the good news to others, and to see that it is 'the power of God for the salvation of everyone who believes'.

If we want to have a proper relationship with God, we must first give our heart to God and make Him our Supreme and Almighty Father. We must have true prayer and communion with God to gain the guidance of the Holy Spirit. Proverbs 4:23 says, *"Keep thy heart with all diligence; for out of it are the issues of life", KJV.* Because man's heart is the temple of God, the most significant rule of practice is to quiet our heart before God in establishing a proper relationship with Him.

Also, if we read God's word regularly, and live in the truth of his word, we can establish a normal relationship with God. God's word is the truth, which can guide us in our way.

*"Verily I say to you, Except you be converted, and become as little children, you shall not enter into the kingdom of heaven" (Matthew 18:3).*

Jesus said, *"I am the way, the truth, and the life: no man cometh to the Father, but by me" (John 14:6) KJV.*

Christ payed the penalty he did not owe, because we owed a debt we could not pay. Repent and trust Christ today, and you too, if you haven't already, can have a relationship with God that will be joy without end, Amen. We thank God for his grace and mercy, that he called us unto his own, and that we have a perfect relationship with him, in Jesus name, Amen.

*Chapter 11*

# SOME QUALITIES AND CHARACTERISTICS OF GREAT RELATIONSHIPS

**Influence**

If marriage would better assist you in serving God, you should seek to be married. You are in the right relationship if that relationship is helping your walk with God and not deterring it. Do you read your Bible more as a result of being in this relationship? Does your partner encourage you to spend time in prayer or are you pressured to neglect personal devotional times with God, so you can be with him or her? Does your partner go to church with you or do they pull you away from church, because they always want to stay out late on Saturday? When your relationship with God is enhanced by your connection to another person, this is a great relationship to be in.

**Respect**

It is a beautiful thing to be around two people who respect each other. You can see it in their eyes, and the supportive tones in which they speak. There is no mistaking mutual respect for any other personal quality, because no other quality looks and acts the same way. Respect is important in any relationship, but you can't respect others unless you respect yourself, and unless they respect themselves. You can admire someone, you can envy them. You can crave their attention. But you can never truly respect them, if they do not respect themselves. People have to give respect to earn respect. Like the saying goes, respect is reciprocal.

## Honesty

One of the most important qualities in every relationship is honesty. If two people are honest with each other, it is the glue of confidence that makes the relationship survive the tests of time. Various circumstances, and conflicts come to everybody, but it is those who are honest with themselves, and their loved ones, who always weather the tests best. Are you in a relationship in which you can tell that the other person isn't being completely honest with you? There's hardly anything else you can discover about your spouse, child, friend, or parent that hurts more than that they're lying to you.

Dishonesty is poison in a relationship. That's because lies never really go away. If you lie, you always know you lied—and that becomes a reality that does nothing but corrode everything it touches. As you hide the lie in your heart, it corrodes everything your heart touches—which means it corrodes everything in your life. Also, you have to tell more lies to cover or explain the lies that you already told. Now who wants to work that hard? There are people for whom; that is not hard work at all. The lies just keep coming!

Be honest in everything you do, and insist on honesty from anyone with whom you share a relationship. This cannot be compromised. Honesty is to a relationship what mortar is to a brick house; without it, you simply can't build. So, building on honesty, is like building on a solid foundation.

## Trust

If somebody respects you, and is honest with you, it is natural that Trust will automatically follow. Trust is an assurance of love. Sometimes however, the Adamic nature in man, may be susceptible to the wiles of the enemy; causing mankind to take advantage of people's trust, in more ways than one. There are many instances in life when people have put their trust on others, and have not been disappointed, however, unfortunately, there has been many other instances where people have put their trust in others; even loved ones, and their trust was crushed so much so, that they go crazy; or almost.

That is why in business, and in other transactions in life, it is not enough to just trust the other party with whom you have a relationship. You're better off putting it on paper, signed and notarized. But you'll be surprised that even with all that, some hardcore dishonest folks still find a way to breach that trust. We hear it on the news just about every day; how various security systems are compromised. The government, big business, private enterprise, your computer, your account, your phone, even your social media outlet, and the list goes on…

God knows about the nature of man. The middle verse of the Bible is Ps. 118:8. Here's what it says:

*"It is better to trust in the Lord than to put confidence in man". KJV*

Printed in the United States
By Bookmasters